Bestial
Box

Judy Older and Louella Odié

SAGE PRESS

Published in 2004

Text and Illustrations © Judy Older and Louella Odié
Design © Sage Press 2004

Set in Palatine italic 10 on 12 point leading.
Display in Palatino Light Italic 48 point.

Graphic Design
Chris Monk of Yellowduck Design Ltd

Text
Judy Older

Illustrations
Louella Odié

Series Editor and Publisher
Mrs Bobby Meyer

Printed in England

ISBN: 0-9542297-8-9

SAGE PRESS
PO Box N° 1, Rye, East Sussex TN36 6HN.
e.mail: sagepress.bm@btinternet.com www.sagepress.co.uk

Bestial Box

As a nation of animal lovers and obsessive gardeners we thought it was time to combine these enthusiasms and introduce some humour into the sometimes-rather serious world of topiary.

Bestial box is not a new idea. Apparently animal topiary cut from box was widely used in Roman times – even in formal Tuscan gardens.

Topiary is certainly enjoying a revival, and a wide choice of clipped box plants is available from garden centres. It is highly unlikely, though, that you will find some of the examples ilustrated in this little book. Our aim is to inspire you to create your own animal sculpture.

Professionals MAY produce perfection, but the amateur can equal this using a large dose of personality and humour.

Do remember that a topiary dog is for life and not just for Christmas, he will need regular feeding and grooming to keep his coat glossy and his ears pricked. If this sounds less fun than the real thing, recall that he will not need walking in the rain, will not shed all over your cashmere sweater nor bankrupt you at the vet.

Best Friends in Box

Before you create your masterpiece in box, there are a number of considerations to bear in mind. Box does grow quite slowly (although **not** as slow as you would think!) so beginning with a substantial plant, to obtain the desired shape as quickly as possible is not considered cheating. If you are starting from scratch consider box hedging plants as your starting point which gives you a greater choice of possible shapes. Otherwise growing on from balls or cones is another simple way to start.

Variegated box is less suitable as there are not many variegated animals

A tightly clipped animal shape invites patting, stroking and hugging, which is why holly is better for geometric shapes. Animal topiary near an entrance or gate is always welcoming, whether it is a single specimen or a group. Try to make it relevant and personal to you and your style of garden.

A pair of territorial cats on either side of a garden gate will have the wiff of authenticity each time you brush by it

Bring out the Animal in Yew

Yew is ideal for large animal shapes as it can make up to eight inches of growth a year when established, and responds well to clipping. Over time it develops a fine textured surface that gives definition to detail. Golden yew would make an interesting contrast mounted on a base of green yew if you wished to create a lion!

Fastigiate yew forms a narrow column when young, and whilst it may need support when young, is ideal for something requiring a neck. For this form of yew to grow in a direction other than upwards it will require coaxing with wire, canes and string. A preformed topiary frame may be easier.

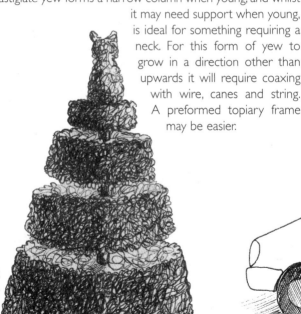

Loose Laurels

Large leaved plants such as laurel, bay and viburnum tinus are ideal for larger animal or bird shapes, but would be too out of proportion for smaller animals, i.e. less than 3ft (1m) in height.

We have successfully grown a speckled cockerel with billowing tail feathers from a spotted laurel, a sitting hen from viburnum tinus and a golden pheasant from elaeagnus.

Use secateurs for trimming and cut right back to the point where the leaves join the stem. Although a good solid base is achievable the effect is soft-focused and textured, rather than the hard-edged detail of smaller leaved specimens such as yew. Do not be deterred by this as the softer blousy effect has a personality of its own.

Animal Discipline

Whilst your topiary will be limited only by your imagination the personality and humour will have added impact if the shape is instantly recognisable. Therefore simplification and sometimes styling is required, and this will come with practice. Whether you are starting with an established plant growing in the garden or a pot bound victim, think of the branches or stems in terms of a skeleton. Which ones are you going to be able to pull and train into the direction you want? Which branches will spoil the line and need removing?

As a general guide we use the leader or strongest flexible stem tied to a stick to make the head end. The bushy ones we train by tying down or back to form the body or tail.

Six year old children are perfectly evolved to simplify any animal into an achievable topiary shape. This may mean your garden becomes full of unicorns, dinosaurs or mystical gremlin

Alternatively you could use ready-made frames, but they are invariably less personal and not quite so amusing. As with humans it is the lumps and bumps that lend individuality.

If you are ambitiously making a four-legged animal, not only will you need four plants with a strong central stem but also bushy branches higher up that will be trained to become the neck, tail and body of the beast. Don't forget that the legs will need to be placed with regard to the finished size of the piece or it will look like it is balancing precariously on a small box.

A more flexible alternative to box plants is lonicera nitida. It will need support if grown over 3' (1m) high as it is prone to floppiness.

Non-standard Standards

A topiary creature made from a box, euonymus or privet standard can either stand alone or be the focal point amongst a mixed border. With only the top of the plant available to trim it is well suited to flying bird shapes or even flying pigs.

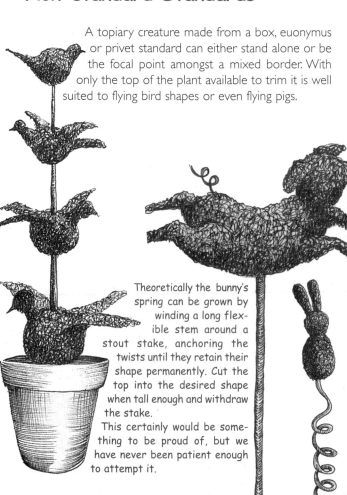

Theoretically the bunny's spring can be grown by winding a long flexible stem around a stout stake, anchoring the twists until they retain their shape permanently. Cut the top into the desired shape when tall enough and withdraw the stake.

This certainly would be something to be proud of, but we have never been patient enough to attempt it.

An adaptation of the traditional Japanese cloud pruning
could become a wonderful colony of nesting birds

Multiple Choices

Using more than one plant to make an individual animal is not that much different to growing a hedge (see page 28), and indeed if you do have a spare hedge hanging about your garden, that is a good place to start.

If no hedge is forthcoming, the final bulk and demeanour of your animal will dictate the number of plants used. Although we advocate cheating and timesaving wherever possible, don't cram together several small plants in order to achieve instant fullness, as you will be storing up trouble for the future.

Much better to live off bread and water for a month and buy bigger plants. As with real animal husbandry, good growing conditions will produce a superior specimen…

Consider the number of changes in direction you want the plant to make and its centre of gravity. Heavy outstretched necks or limbs far away from the centre of a plant will need lots of support to withstand wind damage, in which case several plants may be stronger than one.

High Wire Act

Small leaved dark green ivy is very effective grown against a shed, wall or fence. Use nails to mark the points of your design, dot-to-dot fashion and then wind wire between the nails joining up your picture. Plant one or more ivies at the base and tie in the long trails, trimming the side shoots regularly to encourage denser growth.

Meuhlenbeckia (wire vine), often recommended to hide oil tanks, makes a wonderfully smooth finish when clipped regularly. Grown against a trellis it would be the perfect medium for a large snail.

Ivies and other climbers can also be used three-dimensionally, trained over supported chicken wire or other frames.

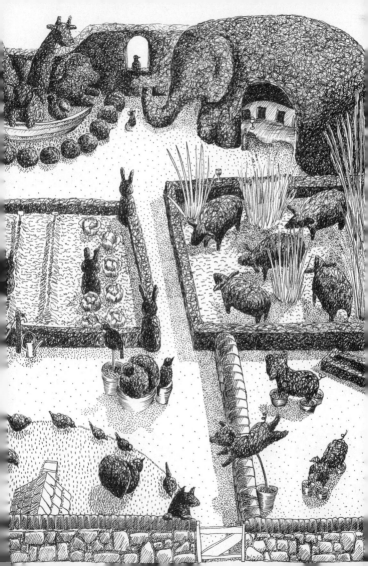

Positions to Surprise Yew

An element of surprise is the essence of a successful topiary garden. These are special places that are all about the journey and exploration. Just as with women if everything is visible in a single glance the voyeur is soon bored.

Turning a corner and coming face-to-face with a 6' (2m) snail clipped from a section of hedge and surrounded by hostas, cannot fail to amuse.

We feel that in every garden there are some sites obviously crying out for a focal point. Topiary has an added element of fun when what at first appears to be a conventional plant or an ordinary piece of trimming metamorphoses into something memorable when seen from a different angle.

The simplicity of topiary is its strength. Don't be tempted to add eyes unless you are aiming for a cartoonish kitsch effect.

Birdial Box

Birds of all kinds are justly popular subjects for garden topiary. Peacocks for instance are often grown for their spectacular tails and are quite easy to develop.

Select a good sized plant with several branching stems. Box, yew or lonicera nitida are the obvious choices but this is also a shape that works well with the larger leaved shrubs such as eleagnus and pittosporum and cherry laurel.

Your plant may be in a pot or already established in the ground.

Push a cane in at the front of the bird at an angle to form the neck. Tie in one or more branches. Clip some of the shoots or branches in the centre of the plant by about half to create the body. The remaining branches at the back of the bird should be angled back and tied to a fan of canes. Trim to encourage other shoots to fill the gaps.

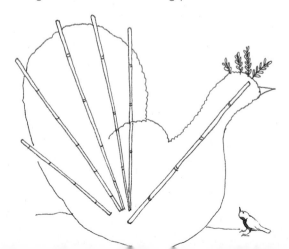

You may need to attach a piece of wire to form the beak.
Other birds may be developed from any plant that is vaguely
spherical. Box balls are commonly formed into hens and
chickens.
A pheasant is formed in much the same way but long shoots
will need to be pulled horizontally and supported on a cane
or wire staked in the body, to give it the typical crouching
stance.

Swans, Ducks and Chickens

A plain wire coat hanger pulled into shape is the easiest frame to use for these birds.

A simple outline is all that is required to bring them to life and box, lonicera nitida or myrtle are suitable subjects.

Chickens are most successful in small flocks of three or five, whilst ducks are very appealing when planted in a line traversing a lawn or field.

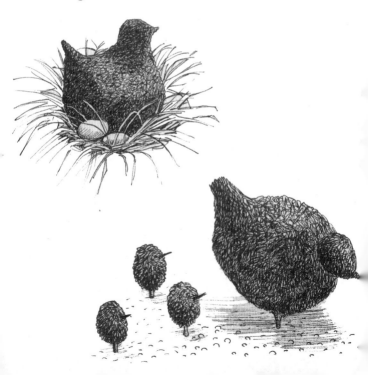

Swans
may
require
a more
complicated
frame but
as a rule
of thumb, anything
curvy requires wire, while
anything straight
needs a bamboo cane. Both
must be tied
in at intervals.

Animals in Reduced Circumstances

If you are restricted to a balcony or windowbox as a showcase for your artistry, then try not to get carried away as ideas flow. Do use only small leaved plants.

One rabbit or a row of rabbits interplanted with herbs would be ideal. Small bushy plants of about 8" (20cm) will fit best, and if they have two strong leaders these could easily be trained into ears, needing very little support. There is no need to worry about feet as these will be covered by the other plants.

Cats or perching birds grown in pots look even better when positioned amongst flowering perennials.

Exceeding the Boundaries
Transforming boring Hedges

Using an established hedge for topiary is a license to be creative on a grand scale. Hedges that are gappy at the bottom are suddenly identified as one or many leggy animals, whereas a more substantial hedge will call to mind more solid beasts. It is your chance to make a dramatic and individual gesture.

Imagine the circus has come to town to perform in the confines of your own garden. You will not annoy anyone if you wish to create a row of elephants trunk-to-tail on your side of the hedge!

Draw the outline lightly on the hedge in spray-paint and then simply cut it to a depth of 3 – 4" (8-10 cms) .Trim the surface, giving it a curved bulbous appearance. If the hedge should have an opening or gate in it encourage or train any long shoots over an arch made from piping. Tie these in and clip them to form trunks meeting in the middle at the highest point. This structure could also be supported on an inexpensive arch frame.

Water Features that do not require Water

Noah's Ark

No need to go to the trouble of a pond for an aquatic theme, and the joy of this particular topiary composition is that it could be created in a sunken garden, a zinc tub, an old bath or indeed an un-seaworthy rowing boat.

Once you have your chosen container planted up, you can get to work creating as many animals as you can possibly squeeze in. Noah himself is an optional extra and so is the dove which could be made from a standard small leaved privet.

Whilst we would advise you against creating this effect in a real pond, we have known it to be done – maintenance could be a chore in deep or cold water!

Collections of topiary on a similar theme are doubly effective if used in a suitable context, i.e. near the seaside.

Topiary for Animals

What about topiary FOR rather than ABOUT animals?
They may not appreciate it but it will cheer you up and make
you realise whether furry or leafy you do have an incurable
obsession.

The Collector's Series of Trees

Are you collecting…?

"… and a very charming book it is…"
Roy Lancaster,
on MONKEY PUZZLE

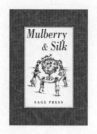

Find us on our new website: www.treefinders.co.uk where you can also take part in the Chequer Tree Survey, exchange recommendations for tree surgeons and read our news stories on the home page. *We look forward to seeing you there.*

SAGE PRESS
PO Box Nº 1, Rye, East Sussex TN36 6HN.
e.mail: sagepress.bm@btinternet.com 01424 774044